To:

From:

Praise for Jamie Madigan's
GETTING GAMERS:

"Jamie takes us as deep into the minds of gamers as is possible without a scalpel. It's a fascinating and essential read."

—NIR EYAL, author of *Hooked: How to Build Habit-Forming Products*

"Jamie Madigan's fascinating exploration of the psychology of gaming blends provocative research findings with lively anecdotes and witty prose. It is accessible, insightful, and a must-read for gamers and game designers."

—NICK YEE, author of *The Proteus Paradox: How Online Games and Virtual Worlds Change Us—And How They Don't*

"Madigan repackages research from familiar names in behavioral psychology such as Dan Ariely, Drazen Prelec, Amos Tversky, and Daniel Kahneman, into delightful yet thought-provoking anecdotes that seek to understand and explain how psychology affects the world of games... Whether you are a game developer or game player, you will likely come away second-guessing pretty much everything about how and why we play!"

—DAVE MARK, President and Lead Designer, Intrinsic Algorithm

"For those interested in the interplay between the science of the mind and the science of game design, there is no better place to begin than with this book."

"Jamie Madigan has put together something fun, engaging, and seriously interesting, and not just for people who love games... I guarantee you will come away from this book with not only a better understanding of human behavior but with advice on how to apply the latest research in your own life and profession.

"For years now, Jamie Madigan has served as the unofficial psychologist of the games industry. If you want to understand how human behavior and games interact, this is the book for you."

THE ENGAGEMENT GAME

Why Your Workplace Culture Should Look More Like a Video Game

JAMIE MADIGAN, PhD

IGNITEREADS
spark impact in just one hour

simple truths®
Small books. BIG IMPACT.

Photo Credits
Internal images © page vi, alengo/Getty Images; page viii, mikkelwilliam/Getty
Images; page xvi, Andrew Soria/EyeEm/Getty Images; page 11, gorodenkoff/Getty
Images; page 20, fergregory/Getty Images; page 30, Kerkez/Getty Images; page 34,
RyanKing999/Getty Images; page 43, RyanKing999/Getty Images; page 48, recep-bg/
Getty Images; page 52, agrobacter/Getty Images; page 56, joe daniel price/Getty
Images; page 78, Rolf Sjogren/Getty Images; page 83, nemke/Getty Images; page 90,
RyanKing999/Getty Images; page 94, adamkaz/Getty Images; page 115, gorodenkoff/
Getty Images; page 120, Mordolff/Getty Images; page 128, Antiv3D/Getty Images;
page 132, Viorika/Getty Images
Internal images on pages xi, 27, 38, 64, 67, 70, 74, 110, 124, and 142 have been
provided by Unsplash; these images are licensed under CC0 Creative Commons and
have been released by the author for use.

Published by Simple Truths, an imprint of Sourcebooks
P.O. Box 4410, Naperville, Illinois 60567-4410
(630) 961-3900
sourcebooks.com

Printed and bound in Singapore.
OGP 10 9 8 7 6 5 4 3 2 1

To Geralyn, Sam, and Mandy
for tolerating me when I won't shut up
about this stuff at the dinner table.

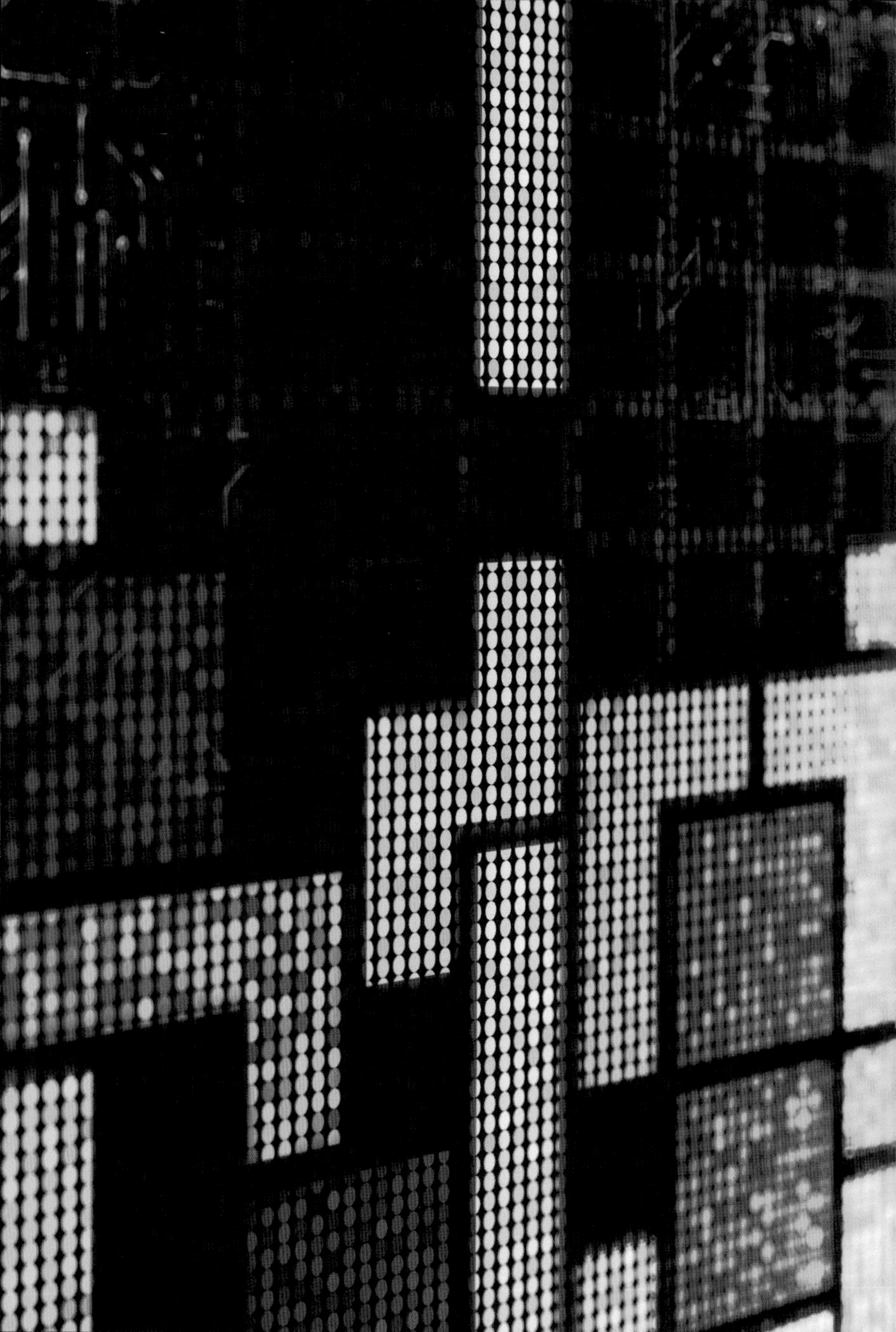

Contents

Introduction

A while back, I was having some trouble with my team. Not my work team, but my teammates in the competitive online shooter game *Overwatch*. "This isn't working," I said, stating the obvious about our repeated failures to assault our enemy's position in the machine shop of Volskaya Industries. There were only a couple of minutes left in the match, so I was feeling some urgency. "Their sniper is really good, and they have a turret in the corner," I said.

"Then change classes," said one of my teammates. It was good advice, so I immediately swapped from Roadhog—a corpulent biker with an asthmatic pig motif—to the hyperintelligent gorilla, Winston. His jump jets would let me bound behind enemy lines and disrupt defenses, but I waited for the rest of the team just outside of the map's choke point before doing so. Charging in alone would be folly.

"Graviton is up!" said another teammate as he joined me, referring to his character's ultimate ability (or in gamer speak, an *ult*) that creates a snarling black hole capable of pulling enemies together into a tight, convenient target. "Winston, take out the sniper and try to get the turret. I'll follow up and pop my ult. Then everybody charge in!"

The plan was a success. I rocketed over the enemy's front lines, chased away the troublesome sniper, and dismantled their turret. My teammate unleashed his Graviton Surge as promised, setting up another player to use D.Va's Self-Destruct ability and obliterate the rest of the enemy team while they were trapped. We won the match with about ten seconds to spare.

My team prevailed in that round of *Overwatch*

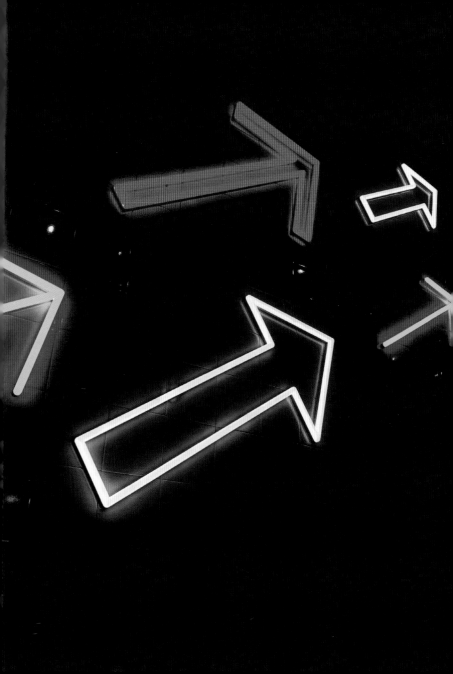

because of our willingness to communicate, adapt our tactics, stay fixated on a goal, and work as a team. We were all focused on the goal and wanted the rewards and character progressions that we knew would come with the win. These are all important behaviors for succeeding in the world of work, which isn't that surprising if you think about it. Both video games and work involve taking in information, adapting to it, sharing it, getting along with people, and persisting toward goals in the service of a shared vision.

Any workplace that was as well-crafted as *Overwatch* would be a wonderful place to work and a *marvel* of productivity. In fact, all workplaces should be more like video games.

Like in any modern workplace, cooperation, continuous learning, hard work, engagement, and a balanced slate of skills are all keys to victory. A lot of this is up to the players to make happen, but the game's designers lay the groundwork, because a lot of thought and science went into engineering the players' experiences.

Accurate feedback about player performance is given *exactly* when it is needed so that the player can get better and understand how the game works. Roles are clearly delineated, and jobs are designed so that they fit together neatly to encourage teamwork and adaptation to the demands of a given situation. Building a team with a suboptimal set of skills will result in warnings and recommendations about what to try instead, and the players often want reasons to keep playing day after day.

This is more important than most people realize, because effective workplaces and popular video games have a lot in common. They both rely on the same underlying psychology of people, teams, and organizations, but sometimes the lessons for *work* are easier to see when presented in the context of *play*. The things that make employees happier, more motivated, and more productive leverage the same underlying psychology that makes video games engaging.

This book will show you how to do this by blending

industrial and organizational psychology (that is, psychological science to improve the workplace) with insights on good video game design. This will help you become a better leader, manager, coach, and coworker given what you know (and are willing to learn) about video games. You don't have to be a hardcore gamer to benefit from this book. It is for anyone looking to create a positive work experience for their team.

Each chapter will apply lessons from the psychology of good game design to topics critically important to managing and leading people in the workplace, such as:

- ▶ How games lay out their tasks, goals, and challenges so that they motivate people to do amazing things

- ▶ The ways in which games encourage problem solving and a growth mindset

- ▶ Why expanding skills, building self-confidence, and finding opportunities to innovate feel so natural to those who play a lot of games

▶ How social information is framed in games so as to engender fruitful competition and cooperation

▶ What multiplayer games can tell us about building cohesive, high-performing teams

▶ How to create shared experiences and values that can craft a great organizational culture and shared expectations for the right kinds of behaviors

Which is all to say that you could learn a lot from video games about how to be an effective leader and manager. **Let's find out how.**

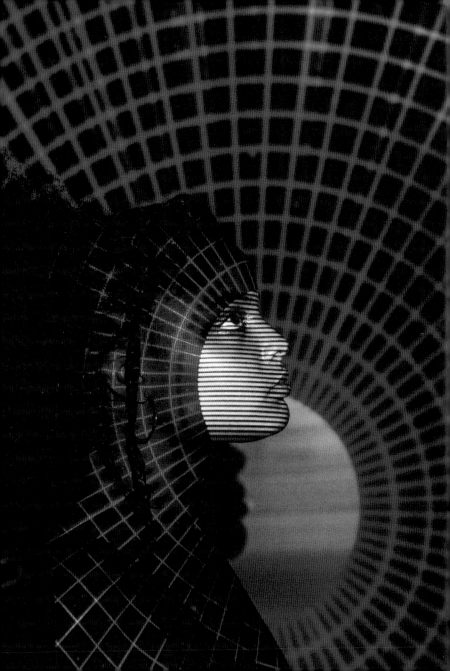

CHAPTER 1

Motivation and Employee Engagement

Have you ever been so committed to reaching a goal that you gave up sleep or sacrificed your free time? So invested and engaged that you persisted over months to complete a massive project that seemed like it would never end? So passionate about an undertaking that you spent *ten years* working on it, with most of that time spent working in secret? Well, a gamer known as Katia Sae did.

Though technically speaking, it wasn't Sae's *job* that

they were committed to for all those years. According to an interview given to the gaming website Polygon, in 2009, Sae began the task of visiting and photographing every star system in the massively multiplayer online game *Eve Online*.[1] They finished the task in 2019, resulting in an online photo gallery containing over fifty thousand screenshots. The massive screenshot collection includes 5,201 systems in Known Space that can be reached simply by visiting stargates, but it also includes an additional 2,604 systems in Wormhole Space that were difficult for Sae to find and dangerous to visit. These hidden systems are connected to Known Space at random points via wormholes that disappear every twenty-four hours and reappear at some other random spot. So Sae had to repeatedly find a wormhole, jump through it, and hope that they ended up in a system that they hadn't yet photographed.

A natural response to this daunting task might be to enlist help, but *Eve Online* is well known for being full of cutthroat players. Bands of such villains will often place spies in other players' groups just to identify easy marks. If they had discovered Sae's peaceful endeavor, many of them would have sabotaged it for their own entertainment or infamy. Don't ask me why, but this is part of the game's appeal for some people. Faced with this additional challenge, Sae had to do much of their exploring in secret and under false pretenses. When they did enlist the aid of in-game colleagues, Sae had to be flexible and creative. Sae found ways to get people to help and co-opted data from search-and-rescue missions to uncover the hidden pathways to missing star systems in Wormhole Space. Sae frequently encountered hostile players, but always got away and kept going.

The task was huge, progress was slow, and Sae could have given up or reduced the scope of their project at any point. But they persisted. When the final screenshot was snapped and word got out about Katia Sae's monumental accomplishment, the developers of *Eve Online* teleported Sae to their own private in-game star system so that final photographs could be taken of a region that was normally completely inaccessible to players. There were cheers from the developers, there were fireworks, and I like to believe that someone brought in a cookie cake or a box of donuts to put in the break room.

Just imagine if you could do for your employees what the designers of *Eve Online* did for Katia Sae and tens of thousands of other players. You can use the same levers as video games to move employees into action and drive engagement.

Researchers have found that highly engaged employees exhibit the following characteristics:[2]

1. **Vigor, which connotes high levels of energy, effort, resilience to setbacks, and persistence in the face of obstacles. Similarly, an employee who pushes through long hours or persists in trying to satisfy demanding customers is displaying her own vigor and energy.**

2 **Dedication**, which is marked by taking a task or job personally, acting with enthusiasm even when cynicism seems reasonable, and taking pride in one's work. Employees demonstrate dedication when they stand fast in the face of setbacks and refuse to back down from commitments because of a sense of personal responsibility.

3 **Absorption**, which is perhaps the concept that most easily comes to mind when we think of someone engaged in work. (Or video games. Especially video games.) Absorption refers to becoming so immersed in our task that we stop thinking about the technology and tools that we're using. We feel like we're in *the zone* and lose track of time as the day speeds by. We've all probably become so absorbed in work or play at one time or another that we were surprised when we looked up to see that quitting time (or even bedtime) was hours ago.

Fostering Engagement through Job Characteristics

In addition to engagement traits, researchers have identified the importance of many job characteristics that tend to create meaningful work—things like challenge, task variety, autonomy, and a sense of how the work fits into the larger organizational context and strategy.[3] Give employees these kinds of experiences through the structure and nature of their work and they will be more likely to experience meaningful work that is *intrinsically* motivating.

This is, of course, easier said than done. What exactly should you as a leader change about your team's jobs so that they can follow the lines from meaningful work to internal motivation to engagement? Well, if you've ever played a video game, you already know at least part of the answer.

Like high-performance workplaces, video games motivate people to keep plugging away at tasks. In fact, video games have to be *more* motivating than work in some ways. Companies offer employees basic, external motivators like a paycheck and a safe work environment. But once those baseline needs are met, additional external motivators are unlikely to drive performance. These kinds of external motivators aren't much of a consideration for video games. Instead, designers have to rely on the same kinds of experiences that every employee longs for and that every enlightened manager wishes they could provide— **meaningful tasks and internal motivation.**

For a specific example, look at *Farming Simulator 17*, which bills itself as "the most complete farming simulator experience." You get to drive around in farming equipment. You get to plant crops like beans. *Beans!* You can plant, like, twenty different kinds of beans! According to its developer, the *Farming Simulator* series is extremely popular among actual farmers and features dozens of authentic brands and scenarios taken from the real world of agriculture.

Or take *Euro Truck Simulator*, which lets you do

exactly what you might guess—drive a truck around Europe. You sit in the cab of a big rig truck and drive through European cities in order to make deliveries, upgrade your equipment, and drive around Europe some more. Ever wanted to be a trucker? Are you currently a trucker? This is the game for you!

These are the kinds of tasks that if you had the chance to do them for hours on end in real life, you'd ask how good the dental plan was first. But it's not that weird if you keep in mind what I've discussed about employee engagement. Let's examine some sources of engagement and intrinsic motivation that video game developers have learned to focus on and how current or future leaders like you can use them to create happier and more engaged employees.

One of the research programs most relevant to gamer engagement was actually started in the workplace: self-determination theory, or SDT.[4] This model explains why someone might voluntarily choose to engage in a task by showing that the characteristics of the task make it interesting, satisfying, fun, or otherwise motivating in and of itself. SDT holds that there are three such task characteristics: competence, autonomy, and relatedness.

1. Competence

Competence is the feeling that you are *good at something*, or at least that you're getting better. Tackling new projects so you can gain experience and take on more and more responsibility is driven by a need for competence. So is beating productivity standards or striving for positive feedback from customers. This feeling of mastery is common in video games, and clever game designers have developed many paths toward it. **A game has to provide a challenge by increasing its difficulty in response to a player's progression and mastery of the game's mechanics.**

Games also have to give players feedback to let them know they're getting better. Scoreboards and leaderboards that show the high scores of racing games, time trials, or point-based games are the obvious examples that have been included in video games since their coin-operated days. It's a clear indicator of mastery if your name or initials are perched at the top of a leaderboard or even if you beat your own personal best record in a racing game like *Forza Horizon* or an endless runner like *Temple Run*. However, other games indicate competence in unexpected and more subtle ways.

Take *Overwatch,* the first-person shooter from Blizzard Entertainment that I described earlier. The game is complex and features dozens of characters to choose from across roles such as offense, defense, healing, and soaking up damage. Winning a match in ranked, competitive modes requires all the players to be competent in their given roles and to play the game well. To facilitate this, Blizzard has baked all kinds of competence indicators into the game. Some are at the most basic of levels, such as getting on-screen indicators of when your shots are connecting. Others are subtler. In the Escort game mode, players must gather around the limousine,

or "payload," of a pompous movie director and escort it to safety. When they begin to move the car forward, their character will call out "I am escorting the payload!" or some other indicator that they are doing what they should be doing. **None of these little touches are accidents or arbitrary.** The game designers include them in order to scratch players' need for competence and show that what they're doing is meaningful.

These design decisions persist into the post-match debriefings. First, one particularly competent player is singled out for a Play of the Game highlight where everyone in the match gets to see him or her do something spectacularly effective. It's kind of like an Employee of the Month award writ small. After that, the competence of select players is highlighted with medals and accolades based on things that they did particularly well. For example, if I was highly effective with the angelic Mercy's ability to patch up her teammates and keep them in the fight, I might get a gold medal for doing the most healing. There are several dozen such competence indicators that you can earn in the course of a match, so many in fact that unless you stood still the entire match, you'll probably be informed of something that you should be proud of every time you play.

If you want to apply what you know about good video game design to motivate employees through a sense of accomplishment, here are some suggestions:

▶ Never underestimate the power of frequent feedback about specific behaviors or outcomes.

- ▶ Celebrate not only successful outcomes but the behaviors that carried people to them.

- ▶ Make clear how those outcomes led to progress toward some goal or higher level metric like team or department performance.

- ▶ Identify employees' strengths and focus performance management conversations on what they tend to do well.

- ▶ Find and share some indicator of progress every day, even if it is small and incremental.

- ▶ Help employees understand and track how much their skills are improving by offering comparative data from the past or having them go through assessments that measure their development over time.

- ▶ Work hard to balance challenging work with the chance to demonstrate competence; work that is too easy does not create a sense of mastery.

2. Autonomy

In addition to mastering skills, video games are about choices. Yes, rules provide boundaries for those choices—rules are what make playing Scrabble something other than an exercise in spelling. But successful games let players satisfy their need for autonomy by giving them a constant stream of meaningful choices, which leads to more motivation and engagement.

To an extent, autonomy can be satisfied by giving players choices in how they move through the game world. Fans of the *Halo* series of first-person shooters often liken their combat scenarios to sandboxes, meaning that they can build the kind of experience they want. Should they saddle up in the Ghost flyer and strafe enemies with laser fire? Or should they head up the middle with a few well-thrown grenades leading the way? Having those choices gets players engaged.

Similarly, autonomy can be satisfied when employees are given the opportunity to manage their own workloads and prioritize one activity over another.

Being given the chance to get creative in how they find and solve problems is another path toward autonomy. Nobody likes being locked into an inflexible system, especially when they know that they could do their job better by relying on their own judgment.

One of the biggest ways that a sense of autonomy is created in video games is through character customization systems and skill development. For example, take the role-playing games in the *Fallout* series. As players complete challenges and gain levels, they are given the option to increase character traits like strength, perception, or charisma, all of which affect the choices they will have for solving future problems. A character with a high charisma will be able to talk his way out of a tense situation, whereas a high strength character can just open fire and more easily survive the ensuing bloodbath. Similarly, letting employees choose what skills to develop is *incredibly* motivating. We all like to have two hands and at least one elbow on our own steering wheel.

Here are some ways for you as a manager or coach to take inspiration from what works in video games when creating a sense of autonomy:

▶ Offer rotational assignments to learn about different business lines or functions.

▶ Encourage employees to cross-train within their own team or functional area.

▶ Let employees choose developmental assignments that play to their strengths.

▶ Allow employees to break from unnecessarily rigid procedures and to process tasks in a way that suits them better.

▶ Create a sense of psychological safety where employees feel that they can make suggestions without fearing repercussions.

▶ Allow or even push employees to take ownership of their own scheduling and methods for doing and tracking work or deliverables.

▶ Solicit new ideas for how to do work or improve processes and allow employees to experiment on small scales or side projects.

▶ Do what you can to increase task variety for employees; doing the same set of things day in and day out presents no opportunity for autonomy!

3. Relatedness

Finally, we have the third intrinsic motivator from self-determination theory—relatedness. We all like to feel that we're important to other people. Games with team-oriented goals scratch this itch, as when players in the online game *World of Warcraft* must work together to defeat a particularly difficult enemy. If your job as the team's tank is to hold the attention of some raging beast and soak up damage so other teammates can do their jobs, you feel pretty important to the group. If you fulfill your purpose, others can fulfill theirs, and your party can prevail. This is especially effective when you know how your tasks fit into the bigger picture of what you and your teammates are trying to accomplish. Similarly, people usually want to know how their work relates to an organization's higher level strategic objectives. Nothing is more demoralizing than working hard on a project or pitching an idea and then having it be ignored or feeling like no matter how hard you work, **nobody will ever benefit from your efforts**.

Relatedness is probably a psychological need that shows up in work settings more than it does in games, even though the latter are becoming more and more social and connected.

But the ways that game designers create opportunities for interactions and relationships among players point to fruitful ideas ready for use by workplace leaders:

▶ Make sure that people know how what they do affects others, not only within their groups but in others as well.

▶ Similarly, highlight how each person's performance affects customers and other external stakeholders, such as suppliers, contractors, or vendors.

▶ Use the job rotation assignments discussed under the Competence section earlier in chapter to give people insights into how their work is interconnected and interdependent.

▶ Consider setting group or team goals that each person can contribute toward, and make it clear how each person's efforts matter.

▶ Publicly acknowledge how individual employees have contributed to meeting important objectives.

▶ Allow access to information or metrics that illustrate how what one person does affects others.

CHAPTER 2

Goals

In 2005, Sony unleashed the first game in its soon-to-be blockbuster *God of War* franchise. In this original *God of War* game, the player controlled Kratos, an extremely angry Spartan who proceeded to grimace and hack his way through most of Greek mythology. For the next thirteen years, that game and its sequels kept the player's objectives fairly simple: *Have Kratos fight stuff. Go as fast as you can. Do as many combo attacks as you can. Don't die.* There were some weapons and items that players could unlock and a few simple puzzles, but in general, it was pretty much a bloody march from point A to point B (or A to β, as it were).

However, in 2018, Sony released a soft reboot of the franchise, which was also called *God of War*. It featured an older, more pensive Kratos who had migrated from Greek mythology to Norse mythology, where the world is apparently much more amenable to player choice and freedom. The game was now substantially more open-ended—so open that players needed help tracking what they were supposed to be doing. So they consulted quest logs, map markers, and progression indicators in ways that were totally different from previous games. While they frequently ripped through Kratos's monstrous foes, players also had to decide which goals they thought were within their grasp, what skill and weapon loadouts they were going to build toward, and what they should do next. Should Kratos find a lost item that would put the ghost of a shipwrecked sailor to eternal rest, or should he hunt for hidden ravens? Also, for the first time in the series, the game gave players feedback about how they were doing and how much they were progressing toward those goals.

This new approach to player performance proved to be extremely popular. The new *God of War* earned high reviews from critics and sold 3.1 million copies in three days, easily making it the fastest selling entry in the entire franchise.[5]

And *God of War* isn't alone. Many games have goals, created with an understanding of human psychology that maximizes the likelihood that players will persevere and improve their performance within the game in order to meet those goals. You can learn a lot from video games about effective goal setting, because game designers originally learned it from the practices of managers and leaders like you.

Goal Setting Theory: Why It Works

Goal setting theory is one of the most well-researched areas of industrial and organizational psychology, thanks in large part to the groundbreaking work of Edwin Locke and Gary Latham. These two psychologists began studying the topic in the 1960s and crystalized their findings in their book *A Theory of Goal Setting & Task Performance.*[6] The gist is that specific, difficult goals increase performance more than having no goals or vague goals like "do my best." There are caveats and nuance, but that's mostly it. Asking someone to make twenty widgets or to collect fifty dragon teeth will result in *more* widgets and *more* dragons on a liquid diet than telling people to just do as much as they can. This is because:

1 **Goals direct the person's attention toward what will help accomplish the goal and away from things that won't.**

2 Difficult goals require more effort than easy ones.

3 Difficult goals require effort over time (i.e., persistence) instead of working hard for a while and then stopping.

4 Goals prompt people to develop better strategies for doing their work.

So when *God of War* players are tasked with defeating a corrupted Valkyrie—one of the most difficult optional fights in the game—in order to collect rare crafting materials, they are more likely to focus on that fight, sit up straight on the couch to put in effort, reload and try again after every defeat, and play around with different equipment and skill combinations to discover what works best.

That all said, there are factors that will affect how much these things will happen. In psychology speak, we call these *moderators*, because they moderate the strength of the relationship between goal setting and performance.[7] Think of these as amplifiers that will make goal setting more effective:

 Goal specificity and clarity

2 **Self-efficacy**

3 **Feedback on performance**

4 **Commitment to reaching the goal**

5 **Complexity of the tasks needed**

The first moderator is the specificity and clarity of the goal. Vague goals like "be among the best in customer support ratings" or "improve the number of goblin corpses on the battlefield" aren't nearly as effective as measurable goals that can be quantified, like "get into the top 25 percent of customer

satisfaction ratings" or "defeat twenty more goblins than the last battle." There's a reason why most video games give players *very specific* thresholds to cross in order to check things off their quest logs or to unlock achievements. As a leader, you can increase goal specificity and clarity by quantifying behaviors or outcomes but also by enumerating the tasks and subtasks to be accomplished en route to the goal.

The second moderator is self-efficacy, which means that the person believes he or she has the ability to reach the goal. Successful video games typically don't ask so much that players think they can't beat a level or progress in the game, and if they do include overly difficult challenges—like beating a level without taking damage—they are far from motivating and rarely accomplished. Similarly, a workplace goal that is clearly out of reach is likely to frustrate employees. They have to believe that if they try hard enough, they can make it. At the same time, too much self-efficacy can backfire and demotivate. Locke and

Latham's research shows that people are motivated by challenging goals. An easy task by definition won't increase performance as much as a difficult one, and people find that conquering hard challenges is more rewarding.

Feedback on performance is also key. People need to know when they are successfully progressing toward a goal; otherwise, they don't know if what they're doing is working. Video games do this by telling players whenever they make progress. If the goal is to score one hundred headshots in *Call of Duty* or collect nine hundred Korok Seeds in *The Legend of Zelda: Breath of the Wild*, the game tells players every time they nudge the needle by filling in some type of progress bar. We rarely have things so cleanly cut in the workplace, but managers should strive to provide regular, accurate, and quantifiable feedback.

Next, a person is more likely to reach a goal when they have goal commitment. This refers to the determination that one uses to pursue an accepted goal.

Players become committed to finishing games or beating a certain level through an emotional attachment or determination to get their money's worth. But we can also see in-game goals with low commitment in the dregs of quest logs and neglected achievements—not to mention the casualties of playtesting, which hopefully get cut before the game ships. Employee commitment to goals can be aided by making sure they know why a goal was set, who it is important for, and what the outcomes will be. Involving them in the goal setting process helps, but research has also shown that a reasonable explanation for why a manager set a particular goal can have the same benefit.

Finally, task complexity matters...in that you want less of it. Think about the way that popular games string players along complex tasks or goals requiring many substeps. *God of War* doesn't expect new players to jump in and beat a beastly troll mini-boss using advanced tactics and nuanced preparation. It first teaches players the basics of combat, then how to upgrade and use various abilities one by one so that they can survive a battle requiring mastery of several game systems. The game broke complex tasks into chunks and allowed players to master them individually. Effective leaders do the same with employees who are working on highly complex goals by providing a road map for how they all fit together.

When Not to Do Your Best

Learning vs. Performance Goals

In the post-post-apocalyptic game *Horizon Zero Dawn*, players have a huge number of things to see, shoot, and do as they help the game's protagonist uncover her curious past and unravel the mystery of why there are robot dinosaurs everywhere. The game really pushes autonomy and choice, so players can do these things in many ways using a variety of game systems. But that can be overwhelmingly complex, even early on. One way that the game designers help players deal with this is through the *hunting grounds.*

These special challenge areas simplify advanced tactics by challenging players to make the best use of their specific environment in order to kill prey as quickly as possible. Based on the goal setting theory that if hunting little robotic deer is the goal, the game should just tell the player, "Hey, go murder twenty Grazers in under two minutes," right?

But *Horizon Zero Dawn*'s hunting grounds don't do that. Instead, they just tell players something like, "Kill as many Grazers as you can." This is a vague, nonspecific goal. Why? Well, the player could just take her bow and start shooting Grazers in the face. That works, tried and true. But what if she instead used her blast sling to start a stampede and then shot out the supports from a big pile of logs so that they rolled downhill and killed a whole herd of the beasts at once? *Yeah! Now we're talking!* At first, this may seem to run contrary to the precepts of goal setting theory as described

above, but to understand why it's not, consider one experiment published in the *Journal of Organizational Behavior* in 2001.[8]

In this study, participants were asked to figure out meeting schedules for multiple people. It was tricky in that it required sorting through information, applying some logical reasoning, and verifying that proposed schedules were free of conflicts. Let's consider two experimental groups from this study:

1 **The *specific, difficult goal* group:** They were told to complete ten schedules in twenty-four minutes, which was known to be difficult but possible.

2 **The *do your best* group:** They were told to produce as many correct schedules as possible in twenty-four minutes.

The study found that people who were told to do their best outperformed those who were given a specific goal. Remember, this was a task that required learning before it could be completed, and there were many ways to go about it. These subjects were committed to the task, optimized their approach, and felt more confidence in their ability to do the task. What's more, a third group told to just develop strategies for the task without worrying about how many schedules they produced did best of all.

When goals don't require learning or discovering new strategies or skills, specific and difficult goals work best. However, when learning strategies are needed so that your team can discover how best to do something, encouraging them to do their best often gets them to optimize their strategies and break down complex tasks into more easily handled subtasks and processes.

So if you want to intelligently take inspiration from video games when setting goals for your team or yourself, here are some things to keep in mind:

▶ Increase employee performance by taking the time to set specific, difficult goals.

▶ Ensure that employees believe that they have the ability to accomplish a goal if they try hard enough; stretch goals should be possible, not outlandishly difficult.

▶ Give regular feedback specific to progress toward goals.

▶ Better yet, automate feedback or give employees access to data they can use as feedback.

▶ Increase goal commitment by involving employees in

the goal setting process or by giving an honest, complete explanation for the goal.

▶ For goals requiring complex tasks, consider setting subgoals or cascading goals that make things seem less complex.

▶ If a task needed to reach a goal remains complex or unfamiliar, consider learning goals, where employees master skills or develop new approaches instead of hitting a performance goal.

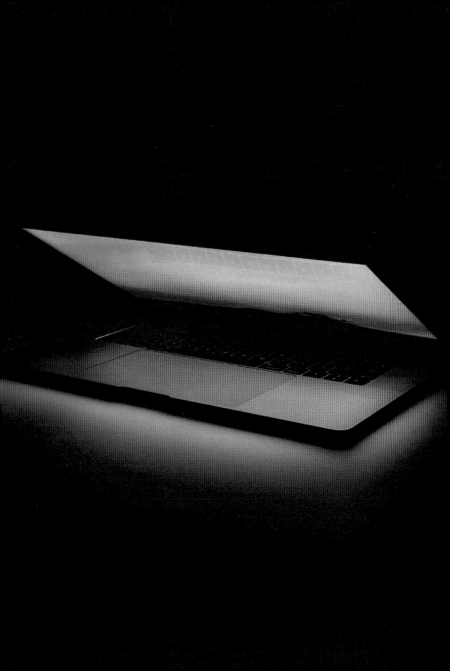

CHAPTER 3
Performance Management and Feedback

Martijn Hols was never quite happy with his Holy Paladin. *World of Warcraft* is a fantasy-themed collaboration where players team up and tackle challenges such as dungeon delving and battling enormous bosses. It offers many ways to customize characters with different classes, builds, equipment, and abilities. How you specialize and play your character matters a lot. Hols, a Dutch software developer, had been playing and tinkering with *World of Warcraft* for years before starting to take it more seriously in 2016. "I was very motivated and trying hard to get better at the game and the spec (Holy Paladin) I was playing," Hols told me in a personal communication. "I joined a guild that was somewhere in the top one thousand and had a lot of fun playing at the hardest difficulty the game had to offer."

But it was challenging play, and Hols needed help improving. His quest to improve his Holy Paladin performance led him to become a regular in an internet chat room with other devoted players willing to give feedback. With their help, Hols soon began fiddling with spreadsheets and analyzing *World of Warcraft*'s logs of what players did during battles. "All of this led up to the point where I really wanted to analyze something that couldn't realistically be analyzed with just a spreadsheet," Hols said. "I'd been thinking about an approach for a while, and after finding out about the Warcraft Logs API, I made a proof of concept." The project quickly expanded beyond the Holy Paladin specialization to pretty much every build the game had to offer and was renamed WoWAnalyzer.

What makes WoWAnalyzer interesting is that it builds on feedback that players already get. Games like *World of Warcraft* have tutorials and give players basic feedback about what they're doing, such as how much damage their attacks are inflicting or if they died because they stood in lava like some kind of moron. But while it's good for beginners and it checks some of the boxes for effective feedback, it's still pretty basic and doesn't speak to how you might use feedback to coach a new employee.

However, with WoWAnalyzer, players get more contextual information, including very specific recommendations on what behaviors to change. A report for a Fire Mage build, for example, might note, "You cast Fireball instead of Scorch when the target is under 30 percent health eleven times. When using Searing Touch, always use Scorch instead of Fireball when the target is under 30 percent health as Scorch does 150

percent damage and is guaranteed to crit your enemy."
(*Crit* means to inflict extra damage.) The WoWAnalyzer
results include reams of insights like this, giving players both positive and negative feedback that is always
constructive and packaged to be immediately useful.
The guidelines that Hols helped put together—the
project now involves dozens of contributors—insist on
"concise suggestions that allow users to quickly understand what potential issues and changes they need to
make to improve." When players look at their results,
they should find suggestions that:

 Explain what was found.

 Make a suggestion that is future oriented.

 Explain why the suggestion is important.

 Suggest a specific, better behavior to take as an
alternative to what the player did.

Control Theory of Feedback

Given adequate ability, commitment, and resources, people generally work hard toward goals. But they also need feedback about how they're doing relative to that goal or the performance standard they're trying to reach. Feedback can come from the environment, from the task itself, or from a manager like yourself. One of the earliest formal theories about using this kind of feedback to motivate progress toward a goal was called *control theory*.[9]

The idea of control theory is that after someone has adopted a goal or set a target for their performance, they use feedback to gauge the distance between where they are (their current performance) and where they want to be (their goal). If they've hit or passed the goal, then great! Celebratory dance time! But if the feedback shows that the person is still short of the goal, then something has to be done. There are generally five reactions to the performance/goal gap:

1 Make a rude gesture and abandon the goal.

2 Stick your fingers in your ears and reject the feedback.

3 Lower your standards and alter the goal to reduce the gap.

4 Work smarter so that you can find better strategies for reducing the gap.

5 Roll up both sleeves and one pant leg, and increase your effort.

Obviously, number four and number five are the preferred outcomes, and subsequent research on feedback has revealed things that you can do to nudge people in those directions. Game developers have also applied these lessons to games in order to keep players happy and to get them to continue in their quests to master game systems and outperform the competition. That's where you, the video game–savvy leader, can help make performance feedback work better.

Give Specific Feedback over General Feedback

How weird would it be if you sat down with a new video game, tapped in some commands on your controller, and the game just said, "You did pretty well, good job!" or even worse, "You did okay, but there's room for improvement"? Unlike most annual performance reviews in the workplace, games simply don't offer vague, nonspecific feedback. You *know* if you defeated the boss, finished the level, or beat the timer. Many games, like the Wild West simulator *Red Dead Redemption 2*, give you scores at the end of missions that are accompanied by checklists of things that you did or did not do. Took longer than ninety seconds to escape the lawmen and left some valuables behind on the baggage car? Yikes, that's going to cost you the gold medal.

Players want to know exactly what they did to get the outcome they did so that they can understand how best to close that performance/goal gap. Similarly, employees are more likely to accept and act on feedback when it's specific. This is a concept that applies to work, training, and education. One 2008 review of the feedback literature, for example, found that "feedback is significantly more effective when it provides details of how to improve the answer rather than just indicating whether the student's work is correct or not."[10] Many of us have suffered through annual performance reviews that amount to little more than a general thumbs-up or a vague recommendation that we do better. That doesn't help us close that performance/goal gap, and we typically shuffle away demotivated.

Focus on Behaviors, Not the Person

A related finding from research on feedback is that people don't like feedback that focuses on them as a person as much as feedback that focuses on their behaviors. As often as they try to make people feel heroic, modern video games don't often just shout, "You're the very best at this! Yaaaay!" Nor do they say, "Wow... You're terrible. I'm embarrassed for you." We don't need nor want this kind of personal judgment from video games, and it doesn't make for very effective

feedback in the workplace either. Feedback providers should know that it's far easier to convince someone to change his behavior than it is to change his self-image, especially for something like work that is important to his identity. Indeed, one analysis of the literature found that feedback interventions that threatened recipients' self-esteem (e.g., by making them feel stupid) were generally less effective than those focusing on behaviors.[11]

The next time you need to provide feedback, recall

how specific Martijn Hols's WoWAnalyzer was with its feedback for Fire Mages. It included feedback about nonoptimal use of the Fireball spell over Scorch in specific situations where the latter would have been more effective. It doesn't just tell the player that they're a bad Fire Mage or that maybe they're not cut out for this game. It gives clear, usable feedback about specific behaviors that were or were not effective.

Give Feedback Quickly and Frequently

Psychologists have long known that the more quickly a reward comes after a behavior, the more likely people are to learn it and repeat it. Sometimes this is hard to do, especially when a manager isn't hovering around, watching everything her employees do. This is why some companies like General Electric are experimenting with app-based performance management tools that immediately crowdsource feedback from everyone around them.[12] Did you like that presentation Toshi just gave? Take out your app, give him a thumbs-up, and write a quick note with some specifics. The team-based shooter *Overwatch* offers something similar, where your teammates can award you endorsements immediately following a match for things like being a good leader, communicating well, or being respectful.

Most successful video games are built around core loops where players see an opportunity to perform, engage in a behavior, and receive feedback immediately (often as a reward). These feedback loops are honed to extreme efficiency through playtesting. Rarely do you have to wait long before getting feedback about something you do in a video game.

Show Progress

The open world game genre largely lets players roam around and do what they want, but such games feature a lot of progress bars. For example, in the *Marvel's Spider-Man* game, every little thing you do counts as progress toward some goal. Stop a mugging and it will increase your progress toward eliminating crime in that neighborhood. Take out this enemy stronghold? That's progress toward undermining a supervillain's power in the city. Capture a wayward messenger pigeon? That falls under "other duties as assigned" in Spider-Man's job description, and you're going to be told about your progress there too.

These kinds of games cram in so many goals and track your progress toward them so visibly because developers have found that showing measurable prog-ress is motivating and will encourage players to keep striving for 100 percent completion. This is true of the workplace as well. In their book *The Progress Principle: Using Small Wins to Ignite Joy, Engagement, and Creativity at Work*, psychologists Teresa Amabile and Steven Kramer had 238 employees from seven com-panies complete daily diaries about how things were going at work.[13] After analyzing over twelve thousand diary entries, the researchers found that the days when

employees reported feeling most motivated, happy, and most engaged tended to coincide with making some progress on meaningful work. Simply inching some imaginary progress bar toward a goal made their day, and experiencing setbacks unmade it. But as Amabile and Kramer point out, managers typically undervalue the impact of such feedback about diminishing the performance/goal gap and neglect to highlight that information in their feedback.

Beyond the Game: What Games Don't Do

The literature on performance feedback is extensive, and while some lessons and inspiration can be drawn from video games, there are some other things that just aren't relevant to the world of games that businesses should still keep in mind.

 Relationships matter. A high-quality and respectful relationship between a manager and an employee will result in more seeking out and using feedback. Trust is especially important, as is a leadership style that focuses on the recipient's personal and professional needs.

 Context matters. Face-to-face feedback is better than email or text.

Setting matters. People prefer positive feedback in public and negative feedback in private.

4 **Individual differences matter.** Some people just like (or hate) feedback more than others and are more (or less) likely to act on it. I'll talk more in a later chapter about different learning orientations and how they relate to feedback.

5 **Organizational climate matters.** By providing expectations and resources for making good use of feedback, some organizations shape employees' feedback seeking and use. I will talk more about climate in a later chapter.

To summarize, here are some things you should do to give feedback more like a video game:

► Keep in mind that you want to help people close the gap between their current performance and their goal.

► Be as specific as you can when giving feedback; avoid generalities.

► Avoid feedback that challenges a person's self-perception or identity; focus on behaviors, not the person.

► Give feedback as quickly and as frequently as you can.

► Help people measure and track progress toward goals; good days are those on which progress is made.

► Give feedback around how people are doing their work, not just the outcome of those efforts.

► *Seriously,* use Scorch instead of Fireball when your target is under 30 percent health.

CHAPTER 4
Growth and Learning

Sometimes our drive for improvement and learning can take us to weird and slightly unsettling places. Consider, for example, the story of a *SimCity* mayor whose relentless pursuit of improvement created a horrifyingly perfect city that was home to over six million souls living under conditions of brutal efficiency.

The *SimCity* series of games challenges players to take on the combined roles of mayor, architect, civil engineer, and just about every other city government job you can think of. *SimCity* mayors cultivate their creations and watch them grow from small hamlets to bustling metropolitan areas by laying down power lines and water pipes, providing services like police and hospitals, and zoning areas for residential or business development. Along the way, they have to deal with citizens' mercurial demands, dial in the right tax rates, choose public policies, and even recover from natural disasters like tornadoes and UFO attacks. Because you can keep tweaking and improving your city as long as you want, *SimCity* games are considered to be the type of game that can't be beaten or finished.

Except someone did.

According to an interview that he gave on Vice.com, twenty-two-year-old architecture student Vincent Ocasla toiled away for almost four years with his copy of *SimCity 3000* and a stack of graph paper that he used to hash out equations to continuously improve his city.[14] Improving in this case meant increasing population density to the maximum that the game's systems would allow. It wasn't easy, and there were many times when Ocasla seemed to come up against an upper limit, but he kept trying to improve.

Planning began in 2006, and developing a design for his perfect city took Ocasla eighteen months of *theory-crafting*—a term used among gamers to describe using mathematical descriptions of a game's mechanics and rules to uncover optimal strategies. There were many false starts and failures, but he took each one as a chance to learn what would and would not work. Each scrapped plan represented something learned, and each new start was a chance to apply lessons learned.

After abstract planning, actual work on the virtual city of Magnasanti took place from 2007 to 2009, using an octagonal design, obsessive micromanagement, and experimentation to get perfection in every pixel. Much of the city doesn't even make sense by the look of it, with eighty-four libraries heaped together on one side and a particularly lonely amusement park huddled in the shadows of looming skyscrapers toward the center. But Magnasanti wasn't designed to look pretty or realistic. It was designed to be efficient according to the game's unspoken rules.

At the end of it all, Ocasla created a YouTube video about the project that is part documentary and part art-house tone piece reflecting the unsettling implications of constructing and living in such a viciously flawless place.[15] (Watch it. It's kind of amazing.) In the video, a chorus chants alarming phrases in Latin over screenshots of air pollution maps and traffic congestion reports, pausing only for vaguely Kafkaesque title cards. You can see page after page of notes, calculations, and aborted attempts at *SimCity* perfection that all culminated in Ocasla's persisting and learning how to beat a supposedly unbeatable game.

There are few better examples of a growth mindset.

Growth Mindset

In your mind, is success about getting better at something, or is it about proving that you're talented? Recall from the chapter on goal setting that there is a difference between learning goals, which encourage people to develop new ways of doing work, and performance goals, which encourage people to do as well as they can. This differentiation has been around for decades, and it eventually evolved into a theory about individual differences in orientation toward either type of goal and about different kinds of performance feedback. Psychologist Carol Dweck popularized this concept in her 2006 book *Mindset: The New Psychology of Success*.[16] In it, Dr. Dweck describes those with a growth mindset as seeing ability as malleable and something to be developed. Effort is the means to improvement. Those with a fixed mindset, however, see ability as something innate and present in fixed amounts. Effort means you lack the talent to do something effortlessly. Fixed mindsets see failure as a signal that you're not cut out for something, while growth mindsets see it as an opportunity to learn and try again. Star athletes, virtuoso musicians, and high-potential leaders often fall into the fixed mindset because they have so much natural talent. But this can lead to more burnout and frustration relative to people who want to continue growing and developing, even without as much natural ability. Dweck summarizes the differences between fixed and growth mindsets like this:

	FIXED	GROWTH
Challenges	Sticks to things that are not challenging (for them)	Seeks to grow through being challenged
Obstacles	Avoids obstacles or quits when encountered	Pushes through obstacles and setbacks
Effort	Sees effort as evidence of lack of talent	Sees effort as required for success
Criticism	Ignores or deflects criticism	Learns from criticism
Success of others	Gets defensive or competitive	Learns from others and draws inspiration

Paraphrased from Dweck (2006) p. 245.

While organizations should certainly value the raw talent and capability that often comes with fixed mindsets, there is a fair amount of evidence that those with growth mindsets are ultimately much more valuable.

One survey, for example, found that those in a work environment defined by a growth mindset were:

▶ 47 percent likelier to trust their colleagues

▶ 34 percent likelier to feel ownership and commitment to an organization

▶ 65 percent likelier to say that their organization supports risk taking

▶ 49 percent likelier to say that their organization fosters innovation[17]

This is great news, because video games teach us to default to growth mindsets. When Vincent Ocasla was trying to create his perfect *SimCity* creation, he hit many natural plateaus and roadblocks. Yet he went back to the drawing board (or graph paper in his case)

and kept trying until he found something that worked. Video games teach you to fail. They even *expect* you to fail.

Here's even better news: mindsets are flexible. They're just beliefs. In her own research, Dweck found that simply explaining how the human brain is flexible and how it can create new connections to adapt to challenges was enough to nudge students toward a growth mindset.

Such a lecture may come off as a bit odd if delivered in the employee break room though, so here are some other recommendations for helping employees adopt a growth mindset at work:

▶ Help employees make specific plans they will carry out when they encounter obstacles and setbacks.

▶ Specifically, use the WOOP (wish, obstacle, outcome, plan) framework from psychologist Gabriele Oettingen to help develop growth-oriented plans.

▶ Encourage employees to ask for help and present managers as a resource for learning.

▶ Reward effort and perseverance, even if they don't immediately lead to results.

▶ Reward self-correction in the face of failure or mishap.

▶ Avoid stereotyping or labeling (e.g., "Operations people are bad at customer service.").

We can see that a growth mindset of the kind required by video games is valuable and encourages people to learn across mediums. But how exactly do video games encourage us to learn? What kinds of qualities and habits do gamers and employees need to develop in order to actually learn from their experiences once they're inclined to do so?

Learning Agility

Well-designed video games get you to try new things. When you face plant into a wall of failure, most games will encourage you to reload and try again with different loadouts, party compositions, weapons, items, strategies, or tactics. When you finally figure out what works, you mark it down in your mental ledger and carry it forward to your next challenge.

Let's take 2016's *Darkest Dungeon* as a specific example. It's a game that seems to take glee in punishing players for not stepping up and putting their thinking caps on. It challenges them to take a party of four adventurers into a sprawling dungeon filled with horrors like Shamblers, Cultists, and Carrion Eaters that are inspired by H. P. Lovecraft tales. Winning requires

experimentation, paying attention to what works, and applying this knowledge to each new problem they encounter. Each dungeon run requires choosing between fifteen different character classes, each of which can be customized with six or more abilities and outfitted with dozens of different items. It's *a lot* of things to learn on the fly. The challenge of the game isn't so much fighting the monsters but analyzing the environment and adequately preparing and outfitting party members to tackle it. Suboptimal choices result in failure, so players spend countless hours experimenting with strategies, figuring out what works, and then finding something that works even better. The game *demands* that kind of investment.

This kind of ability to persist and learn has also caught the attention of organizational psychologists who study what makes for successful leaders, though they usually don't mention eldritch horrors specifically. (Not often, anyway.) Researchers Michael Lombardo and Robert Eichinger kicked off the modern conceptualization of this kind of ability to learn quickly in 2000 when they coined the term *learning agility*.[18] In that article, they posited that successful leaders are those who learn more effectively and are able to be more flexible in novel situations.

In the nearly two decades that followed, the popularity of learning agility exploded, and companies came to realize that they needed people who could roll into a strange situation, figure out what to do based on previous experiences, and chart a path forward. This, as opposed to people who would just look around, throw up their hands, and shout "Ha, nope!" One survey found that 62 percent of organizations consider and try to measure learning agility when hiring, making it by far the most commonly considered quality for aspiring managers and other leaders.[19] Tools that measure the construct go by varied names like viaEDGE, Talentx7, and the Burke Learning Agility Inventory. Each model is slightly different in the number of facets to learning agility it claims exist, but all of them generally measure the same set of things.[20]

Personally, my favorite model of learning agility comes from the Burke Learning Agility Inventory, mostly because its list of subscales maps best on to the way gamers display and develop learning agility while playing games. I'm pragmatic that way. Those subscales are:[21]

 Flexibility—being open to new ideas and proposing new solutions.

2 **Speed**—acting on ideas quickly, so those that aren't working can be discarded and other possibilities accelerated.

3 **Experimenting**—trying out new behaviors, approaches, and ideas to see what is effective.

 Performance risk taking—seeking new activities, tasks, and roles that provide opportunities to be challenged.

5 **Interpersonal risk taking**—discussing differences with others in ways that lead to learning and change.

6 **Collaborating**—finding ways to work with others that generate unique opportunities for learning.

7 **Information gathering**—using various methods to remain current in one's area of expertise.

8 **Feedback seeking**—asking others for feedback on one's ideas and overall performance.

We see these kinds of qualities encouraged and even required in many video games. Players need to be flexible and experiment with different kinds of approaches for in-game problems so that they can gather information about what approaches work best.

Given all these strategies, here are some things you might try as a leader to encourage learning agility and to develop it in yourself:

▶ Encourage and reward flexibility and creative solutions to old and new problems.

▶ Put people together in new configurations so that they can learn from one another and get exposed to new ideas.

▶ Require people to seek out new sources of information when they encounter a problem; don't rely only on what's readily available.

▶ Have employees develop areas of expertise, then task them with sharing that expertise and building new experts.

▶ Don't hide from discussion of differences in how to do things; embrace them and encourage people to share them.

▶ Make people experiment with new things, even if they don't always work out.

CHAPTER 5
Competition and Cooperation

Throughout part of the summer of 1992, the world's best athletes climbed the awards podiums for their respective events in the Summer Olympic Games held in Barcelona, Spain. The gold medalists were often radiant and grinning into the cameras, having proven themselves to be the best of the best. *But forget them.* Everyone understands why they were so happy. It was the silver and bronze medal winners that researchers from Cornell University and the University of Toledo were really curious about.[22] One would expect that the higher someone finished in the Olympic ratings, the happier they should be. Gold should be happiest, silver second happiest, and bronze third happiest. But that didn't seem to be happening. The researchers looked closely and saw that, on average, the silver medalists standing up on their podiums at the awards ceremonies were *not nearly as jubilant* as the third-place bronze winners. Why not?

Human psychology is complex, and there's a lot more going on between people's ears than you might expect during a competition. People consistently make irrational comparisons with others, they obsess over missed opportunities, they react differently depending on how comparisons are framed, and they obsess over arbitrary performance standards. To understand what happened to the silver and bronze medal winners in the 1992 Summer Olympics, we need to understand things that video game designers have figured out that get people to engage in friendly competitions and motivate them to keep trying until they're satisfied with their performance—and how employers do the same.

Many of these psychological principles in play were born of research in social and organizational psychology. We don't often think of our own employees challenging one another, but the fact is that they sometimes compete for opportunities, promotions, and resources. Even if they eschew head-to-head competition, employees compare their own performance against standards or their past performance. As a manager, you have a chance to frame, communicate, and present performance information that promotes friendly competition and the engagement that comes with it.

In other words, you can learn a lot from video games about how to get people to compete and work harder—and to *be happy* while they do it.

Leaderboards and Goals

Leaderboards that rank people in terms of their performance are a standard ingredient of both video games and attempts to make workplaces more gamelike. It's not uncommon in either situation to see your name alongside others on a big, glowing list that shows who is doing the best at whatever game or task its creators have deemed important. Video games are full of leaderboards. The online shooter *Fortnite*, for example, shows the player a leaderboard of where he or she ranks among either all the other players in the world or his or her friends. The platforming game *Mega Man Legacy Collection* has a speed-run challenge mode with its own set of leaderboards where players try to complete levels as quickly as they can. Even the Olympic medals ceremony can be seen as a three-person leaderboard. Leaderboards are a simple and common idea that people tend to like. But in what situations are they more likely to work?

One study by Richard Landers, Kristina Bauer,

and Rachel Callan suggests that it has to do with one of the concepts we've already discussed—goal setting theory.[23] The researchers split subjects up into groups and had them complete a standard creativity task where they generated as many possible uses for a simple knife as they could. Each group was given a different kind of goal: an easy goal, a difficult goal, a practically impossible goal, and a goal to simply do their best. A fifth group was given no goal but was shown a leaderboard full of initials and scores that corresponded to the different goals of the other groups. As they completed the task by thinking up and typing in uses for a knife, participants saw their initials move up the leaderboard in real time. With this approach, the researchers hoped to find out how effective leaderboards were relative to setting goals, which was already known to increase performance.

Results showed that competing with those on a leaderboard spurred people to perform better than those who set easy goals or who were told to simply do their best. In fact, they performed on par with those who set difficult-to-impossible goals. This suggests that leaderboards—be they in a video game or in the workplace—operate by *getting* people to set goals. But it also suggests that this is most likely to happen with simple tasks where the person can see a straight line from their efforts to reaching the goal. Leaderboards for complex tasks like *developing your employees* or *identifying competitive threats in the business environment* are unlikely to do any good. The authors of this study emphasize the moderating role of goal commitment by pointing out that people have to buy into the comparisons made by looking at where they are on the leaderboard relative to others. The authors note that "if people do not believe a leaderboard provides worthwhile goals, leaderboards will not be successful at altering employee behavior."[24]

So this can be tricky if you're implementing leaderboards as part of a gamification effort. You need to make sure that people naturally and willingly accept the goals implied by the social comparisons in the leaderboard. Fortunately, this is one of the things that video game designers have put a lot of effort into, and there are several theories from psychology that can help.

Social Comparison Theory

Imagine that a consultant has come in and gamified your workplace, instituting a system where you earn points for doing various parts of your job well. For extra effect, she also hung up a picture with a kitten dangling from a tree branch above the caption "Hang in there!" At the end of the week, you get a notification saying you have scored 348 points. You sit at your desk, gaze at the picture of the imperiled cat, and wonder, "Is that…good?"

A long line of research in social psychology has established that we like to know how well we're doing, be it in life, work, or games.[25] Leon Festinger and his students created and refined social comparison theory

during the 1950s, which states that if we can't get useful, objective information about our performance or standing, we look for the next best thing: comparing ourselves against others. But we don't like to compare ourselves to just any random stranger or the most successful person in the history of our profession. We like to make these social comparisons against people who are similar to us in ways related to the task or job at hand—people with similar experience, age, backgrounds, and access to resources, and who should be trying about as hard as we are.

This is why video game developers long ago figured out that global leaderboards comparing a player's score against the best players in the world were not all that motivating. When you're struggling to complete a race track in under three minutes, it's not too motivating to know that "xXFastd00d96Xx" somehow did it in twenty-two seconds and that he's nine thousand places ahead of you in the rankings. What's much more motivating is to know that you're only six seconds away from beating your friend Ravi's high score. Or that your other friend Tina just beat your score by two seconds. Beating them is a goal you can commit to, because you know your friends and you know how similar they are to you. Similarly, leaderboards that highlight other similarities, such as amount of time played, character classes played, or geographical location, can be even more motivating, because they facilitate social comparisons that are more meaningful. This is something to keep in mind as a manager facilitating social comparisons, whether it's in gamified situations or not. You should help people understand why these comparisons are relevant and how the other people are similar. Otherwise, you risk having people dismiss them and not use that information to set performance goals.

But it's not only who's in the group that you're getting performance information on. The length of the leaderboard also make a big difference, because we feel differently about our performance depending on where it places us within our frame of reference.

Big Fish, Little Pond

The competitive, online shooter *Apex Legends* has a pretty simple premise: drop onto an island with a bunch of other players and fight to the virtual death. The game forces players to group up into three-person squads that compete with nineteen other teams of the same size. I am not particularly good at the game, so

I tend to have a lot of time to look at the *squad elimi-nated* screen that pops up when your squad gets wiped out. This screen shows where your squad ranked over-all (e.g., eleventh out of twenty), but it also shows how you stack up against your squad members in terms of the number of enemies you eliminated, the damage dealt, and how long you survived.

This screen makes me think of leaderboards and a phenomenon called the *big fish, little pond effect*. The gist is that those who are ranked at the top of a poorly performing group tend to feel better about their per-formance relative to those ranked near the bottom of a highly performing group.[26] Like the high school vale-dictorian who is used to being the smartest person in his school but then gets in to a competitive college where he's thoroughly average. Being in a small pond makes us feel like a big fish. **We like that**. People who see they did better than their downed squad mates in *Apex Legends* might have preferred to win the whole battle royale, but they get some satisfaction from seeing that they were the best in their group. Similarly, someone in a squad that placed much higher in the rankings might be less happy if they were the worst of their three-person group.

Similarly, as a manager, you should keep the big fish, little pond effect in mind when creating leaderboards or other social comparisons, especially if your goal is to foster motivation and friendly competition. Make results available by department or team instead of just by division. Appropriately celebrate the people who are the best of the best, but also give others a chance to compare themselves to their immediate teammates.

Given all this, if you're implementing leaderboards or some kind of rankings to your workplace in an effort to motivate your employees, here are some things to keep in mind:

▶ Having global or division-wide rankings is okay, but you should also allow people to filter down to their own team level or the cohorts of their choosing.

▶ Invoke the big fish, little pond effect by finding ways to cut the views so that people can see how they're doing well (or how they can improve) within a smaller group.

▶ Facilitate more meaningful social comparisons by giving people information about those near them in the rankings or by highlighting peers and counterparts on other teams.

▶ Encourage employees to set goals around climbing to specific places in the rankings and help them get there by keeping everything from previous chapters about goal setting in mind.

Competing against Ourselves

In golf, every shot matters, right? Especially in highly competitive tournaments like the PGA Tour, golfers can slip down the rankings on the basis of just one or two shots. Given that, one would assume that these extremely motivated players put maximum effort into every stroke, from the first drive to the last putt. Yet researchers from the University of Chicago and the Wharton School of the University of Pennsylvania had their doubts. They examined 2.5 million shots made by professional golfers to see if it mattered whether or not a shot would push a golfer above par or below it for a given hole.[27] What they found was that golfers were more likely to take extra care and sink a shot if it kept them from going over par, relative to identical shots that wouldn't affect their over/under par results. But if total number of strokes is what determines a tournament winner, this is irrational; **maximum effort should be made on every stroke.**

Maybe in the future, some completely rational golf robot will play that way, but in the meantime...we're all human. This golf study is just one example of how arbitrary goalposts can affect our motivation and thus our performance, both in play and on the job. Another researcher had people act out the role of CEOs and experimented to see if the arbitrary cutoff of having

them appear (or not) on the Fortune 500 list would affect how likely they were to cooperate on a mutually beneficial joint venture with another company.[28] The trick was that the joint venture would benefit the other company more and cause it to swap places with the subject's company on the list. The researcher found that people were far less likely to cooperate if it meant going from 500 to dropping off the list, relative to experiencing the less psychologically meaningful change of going from 103 to 104.

These effects are important, because sometimes we don't compete against other people so much as we strive to surpass some standard or cross some threshold. If your company invokes cutoffs for making an all-star list or being in the top 10 percent of performers in a gamified system, people at the edges of those lists are going to be a lot more motivated, because not all rungs on a tournament ladder are equally spaced. Dropping from 10th to 11th is a lot worse than moving from 8th to 9th or 111th to 112th.

This is, in effect, the answer to the mystery of what happened to those Olympic silver medalists. It's why they appeared less pleased with themselves than the bronze medalists. Silver medalists were making upward social comparisons against people with gold around their necks. The counterfactuals they had on top of their minds were about how if they had tried just a *little* harder, they would be the best of the best. Which can be kind of upsetting. But the bronze medalists weren't thinking about how close they got to gold. They were elated that they had pushed themselves hard enough to avoid not getting an Olympic medal at all.

If you are implementing a gamification system with points or setting standards for people to perform against at work, here are some things to keep in mind:

▶ Make sure that standards are clear and that people know what's required to participate in whatever version of an Olympic medal ceremony you have.

▶ If your goal is motivation, add rungs to the tournament ladder by including multiple cutoffs in the distribution, and recognize people for hitting all of them.

▶ Pay special attention to people who are close to moving ahead of or behind recognized cutoffs for performance, as they will be particularly motivated to improve.

▶ Don't underestimate the effect that surpassing a performance standard can have on someone and how it might motivate them to compete in such a way that undermines their ultimate goal (and that of your team).

CHAPTER 6

Teams

The competitive, team-based game *Heroes of the Storm* is popular among casual players, but in the past, it also had a thriving tournament scene. As with other games in the genre, like *League of Legends* or *DOTA2*, tournament-level *Heroes of the Storm* requires five-person teams to know all the ins and outs of every one of the almost one hundred heroes available for play. Knowing how they complement one another, how they counter enemy picks, and how they interact with every map's objectives is key to success, and blind spots in that understanding can lead to some pretty spectacular tournament upsets. In the 2017 Heroes Global Championship midseason matches, teams from North America weren't putting up a very good show. The most favored was a team going by the name Roll20, but even they were expected to lose early in the brackets. Probably in their first set of matches against MVP Black, a former championship team from Korea.

As you can probably guess from the underdog setup, things did not go as everyone expected, at least in the first match of the series. When MVP Black failed to prevent Roll20 from choosing its preferred team of five characters, the North American team had a chance to play with the combination of characters that suited it best. The cornerstone of their team was a pairing of Medivh, a mage who can summon gateways between points on the map, and Diablo, a brutish demon who can pin down individual foes. Roll20's star player controlled Medivh and used that hero's teleportation gates to devastating effect. In every play, everyone on Roll20 seemed to know exactly what to do and could anticipate how the enemy team was going to respond. Time after time, Medivh would gate Diablo around so he could peel away MVP Black's defenses without missing a beat. Roll20 won the game not only without losing a single structure but without even a single death. It was a remarkable and memorable accomplishment for tournament level play, all because the Roll20 team was so in touch with one another and understood the flow of the match so well.

Team Cohesion

As more companies have started to rely on teams to perform complex or difficult work, research on teams and small groups has steadily expanded and attempted to enumerate all the factors that affect team performance.[29] Team size, diversity, conflict, empowerment— they've all been studied. However, team cohesion is frequently cited as one of the most important predictors of team performance, going back all the way to the 1950s when it was conceptualized as the forces that compel people to remain part of a group.[30] That concept eventually grew to be more multifaceted and to include two types of cohesion:

 Social cohesion

 Task cohesion

Social cohesion has to do with how attracted people are to one another in the group. Not necessarily in the Ohmygosh-Brad-is-so-handsome sense, but more of a general liking of the people in your group and a desire to be around them. If your team goes out for bowling after work or forms a *Counter-Strike* league, it probably has a lot of social cohesion. *Task cohesion*, on the other hand, describes members' willingness to work together on group tasks or in service of reaching group goals.[31] It's basically group task commitment, which is a concept you will remember from the chapter on goal setting and that has been found to be more important than social cohesion for predicting team performance.[32] And that's pretty much the punch line here—whether you're talking about group or task cohesion, highly cohesive teams tend to perform better.[33] Thankfully, there are a few things that researchers have identified that impact how you can create cohesion and leverage this cohesion/performance relationship.

The first is establishing group-level tasks and goals much in the same way that you would to create commitment to individual goals. But keep in mind that you should not create conflict between an individual's goals and the goals of her group. You used to see this in video games before developers got more savvy about designing achievements. Players would often be challenged to earn an achievement by getting so many grenade kills or riding in vehicles for certain distances.

This was fine, except when driving a tank in circles for the whole match didn't exactly align with the team's goal of winning.

Another factor is group size, in that smaller teams tend to be more cohesive.[34] Smaller groups have a better chance to get to know one another and develop bonds of social cohesion. They also allow teams to avoid behaviors that will undermine cohesion, such as social loafing—a term psychologists use to describe shirking and reducing efforts because you assume someone else will pick up the slack. Think about video games with massively large teams like Sony's *Planetside 2*, an online shooter where factions have literally thousands of players on the same team. These make for some pretty spectacular battles over territory on a continental scale, but it does little to make players feel like any kind of cohesive unit relative to a game like *Destiny 2*, which organizes players into much smaller clans or even fire teams of only six people. Players in huge teams don't feel much cohesion with their teammates, but those in much smaller, persistent guilds typically do. Players in huge groups are also more likely to fall prey to what psychologists call *deindividuation*, where they feel less like an individual player and more like a lonely cog in a larger machine that can't be held accountable for its actions.[35] Besides all that, research has shown that people *just like* being in groups better when they're smaller.[36]

The next and probably most important factor that impacts how effective cohesive teams will be is the interdependence and level of interaction required to complete the team's work. Teams with low task interdependence don't involve much specialization, sequencing of tasks, or reliance on others. In highly interdependent teams, members have to wait for others to perform their part of a process before they can do theirs, and the work that they do can easily impact others.

Ascending levels of team task interdependence can be described as:

▶ Pooled

▶ Sequential

▶ Reciprocal

▶ Intensive[37]

Pooled interdependence is hardly interdependence at all, as members just work on pieces of a task until it's all done. A simple team death-match mode in *Destiny 2* features pooled interdependence, because each member of the five-person squad just tries to rack up kills until one team's total is enough to win. *Sequential* workflow is when tasks move from one team member to another without any back-and-forth. In the frantic kitchen simulator *Overcooked*, for example, players can experience sequential workflows when one chef chops vegetables and then passes them off to another chef to incorporate into a stew. If that stew then gets handed off to the first chef so that she can finish it off, the interdependence has become *reciprocal*.

Intensive workflows, however, are the kind that we most often see in multiplayer video games. They happen when work can flow between multiple team members and everybody has to be on top of their game to succeed. This is the kind of extreme inter-dependence you saw in Roll20's *Heroes of the Storm* match where Medivh helped Diablo dance in and out of portals while the rest of the team defended and completed map objectives.

If you are a manager or other leader who wants to increase team cohesion in the hopes of improving performance, here are some things you might try:

- ▶ Enhance team commitments to tasks through team-oriented goals, but don't create dysfunction and conflict by having these team goals conflict with the goals of individuals.
- ▶ Limit group size where possible.

▶ Create interdependencies, then make sure that team members understand those interdependencies and how their work performance impacts others.

▶ Don't expect cohesion to happen immediately; it can take time and exposure.

Shared Mental Models

Some games don't require players to grasp a whole lot of complexity. *Fortnite*'s battle royale mode, for example, isn't complex, even when players are on teams. *Shoot the other teams. Don't die.* That's mostly it. But some other games are far more complex, feature much more interdependence, and much more strongly illustrate the cognitive aspects of teamwork.

To compete at the highest levels of the tactical shooter *Tom Clancy's Rainbow Six Siege*, for example, a player has to not only understand the role of their hero but also how it interacts with any of the other fifty-two operators that teammates or opponents could choose, and once in a match, they need to track what's going on in terms of what objectives are active, what the enemy team is doing, where their teammates are, what special abilities they have ready, what talents all the other players have chosen, who is currently alive, and more. The answers to all these questions form a complex decision matrix that players must use to perform well. The operator Castle can deploy armored panels that can lock down any doorway, but an attacking player using the operator Thermite can place fiery exothermic charges that can burn through such barriers. But if the barrier has been energized with electricity by another operator, then the exothermic charge will be destroyed before it can do its work. The game's developers designed these interplays between environments, objectives, and operators to make teamwork challenging but extremely rewarding for groups that can keep everything straight in their heads.

Organizational psychologists call this idea *mental*

models. These are organized mental structures that allow people to predict and explain the behavior of the people around them, recognize and recall relationships among things in the environment, and create predictions for what is likely to happen in the future.[38] As with cohesion, recent researchers have focused on two types of mental models in the context of teamwork: *task-focused* and *team-focused.*[39] The first deals with tasks and technologies available to the team. Does each team member understand the equipment, technology, procedures, and environments likely to be in play and necessary to complete the team's work? The second type of mental model deals with team members. Do members understand everyone's roles, responsibilities, and work interdependencies? Do they understand what the other team members possess in terms of knowledge, expertise, skills, and preferences?

Both types of mental models are critical for team performance. If you're a pharmaceutical company account manager working with doctors to make sure that patients take their medicine regularly and don't quit treatment, you should have a mental model of how doctors are prescribing the drug, what kinds of hardships or bad habits lead patients to stop taking it, and what patients have to do to secure refills, just to name a few things. If you're on a team along with a physician, a home care nurse, and a social worker, you all need mental models that overlap. These shared mental models allow you to make sense of the patient's world, the task of getting them to stick with a treatment, and what each member of that team needs to do toward that goal.

These shared mental models are even more important when team members cannot freely and frequently communicate or strategize ahead of a task, such as with surgical teams reacting to emergencies, soldiers encountering an ambush, or *Heroes of the Storm* players pushing a map objective. Having a shared mental model alleviates the need for communication and planning, because team members have a strong idea of what's going on and what others are likely to do.

Some research has found that it's also important to employees who telework, because they don't have the same opportunities for face-to-face communication and coordination as their on-site peers.

If you want ideas for how to help your team develop shared mental models, look to video games. Game displays often give indications of when your teammates' special abilities are available, for example. Watch any pro *Overwatch* player and you'll see them constantly tapping the tab key to get this information from a subscreen. The battle royale game *Apex Legends* has an elaborate ping system that sidesteps verbal communication altogether, allowing players to simply aim at an item or location and tap a key to issue a context-sensitive alert about the presence of an item, warnings about enemies, or suggestions to explore an area. Death cams in most online shooters zoom in on whoever just killed you, letting you know about how your foes are using the map and their abilities. And, of course, games will offer an endless stream of on-screen and in-ear updates about the status of the match and other players, which you can plug in to those mental models as you develop them.

These kinds of examples of how to build shared mental models are everywhere, and here are some specific suggestions for applying them to the world of work:

▶ Use team debriefs after projects or milestones to discuss team strengths and weaknesses and how people lived up to their responsibilities.[40]

▶ Give employees dashboards that give them access to information about what their teammates are doing and the status of their work.

▶ Have discussions with pairs or other small subsets of the group to talk about each person's priorities, strengths, and shortcomings.

▶ Allow team members to give feedback to one another and discuss what they need.

▶ Promote at least some level of cross-training so that each team member understands what the others do.

CHAPTER 7
Culture and Climate

The ridiculously popular *League of Legends* from Riot Games—which by some estimates has 111 million active players and made $1.4 billion in 2018[41]—has for a long time had trouble with *toxic behavior* among its players. To help deal with these toxic players, Riot created a Player Behavior Team full of cross-disciplinary experts who put together systems, procedures, rewards, and punishments to help shape its community. This team implemented a reputation system that rewarded honorable player behavior, for example, and experimented with changing the social dynamic of its five-person teams by seeding it with pairs of friends who were more likely to be nice to each other.[42]

But Riot's problems with toxic behavior apparently weren't limited to its players. In late 2018, the gaming website Kotaku released a story that had been taking shape for years as one of its reporters interviewed current and former Riot employees.[43] Those sources alleged that Riot had a toxic environment on this side of the screen as well. They said that it was a workplace that systematically put women at a disadvantage during interviews and team meetings by assigning more value to experiences that they were less likely to have and rewarding workplace behavior that was extremely aggressive and assertive. In response to these allegations, the California Department of Fair Employment and Housing launched an investigation into Riot's employment practices and the possibility of sexual harassment.[44] The stories coming out of

Kotaku's reporting also described a "bro atmosphere" that encouraged juvenile and sexist behavior, such as laughing when the company's chief operating officer walked into a room, backed up against someone, and passed gas directly on them.

That's right. You're reading a business book that just described a C-suite leader who farted on his employees. *I'm so sorry.* But bear with me, because you could learn a lot from this video game company about how to create (or recreate) and maintain a strong corporate culture.

Organizational Climate

But first, let's pause for a quick discussion of that *culture* term. In most cases, people use *organizational culture* to describe people's understanding of what things are expected, tolerated, and punished in a workplace. But because organizational psychologists like splitting hairs and being fussy about definitions, we use the term *organizational climate* to describe that concept. So that's the term I'll use for the rest of this chapter.

The authors of one 2013 review of the literature defined organizational climate as "shared perceptions of and meaning attached to the policies, practices, and procedures employees experience and the behaviors they observe getting rewarded and that are supported and expected."[45] A pithier definition is simply "the way things are done around here."

Organizational climate results from leader behaviors and personnel practices (e.g., hiring, compensation, or training), but it's the shared meaning people attach to these things that we're really talking about. Climate emerges over the natural course of work and as a result of interactions within the workplace.[46] For example, promoting people who yell in meetings or only hiring people who can talk at length about what kinds of video games they enjoy.

Early research on organizational climate focused on a general concept of how much an employer cared

about the well-being of its employees, but in recent years, researchers have been trying to figure out specific types of climate that emphasize certain internal procedures or outcomes. Climates that result in worker safety and customer service are the most frequently studied, but climates for diversity are also common.

Understanding how to develop these climates is still an ongoing research topic, but it's clear that the formal personnel practices that you as a leader design or at least implement play a big role. At one point at Riot, interviews would include questions about what video games the job applicant played, with special emphasis on the company's own *League of Legends*. If candidates didn't answer in a way that made them seem like a hardcore gamer (however the interviewer chose to define that), then it raised concerns over whether that person should be hired, no matter what job they were applying for. In a 2018 interview with *Variety*, one of Riot's cofounders said that "we hire gamers and only gamers," because it supported his desired climate of a focus on players.[47] This happened even if a person was applying for a job in accounting or some other area where gaming experience was wholly irrelevant.

Riot also tended to promote people who argued the most energetically and assertively for their ideas in the hopes that the best ideas would win out and their champions could be put in a place to implement them. This led to a lot of interpersonal conflict and demands that the other person develop a thick skin, because people shared this understanding of how to get ahead. Unfortunately, this also meant that many women were at a disadvantage, either because they were less aggressive or they faced a double standard when they were just as vociferous as their male colleagues. However, the same concept can be applied to climates that are more universally positive. Research on climates for workplace safety, for example, has highlighted the importance of requiring safety training and promoting based on individual safety records for creating a climate for safety, which then reduces accidents and injuries.[48] People see that safety-conscious behaviors are expected and rewarded, so they don't take risks or work without protective gear.

Beyond human resources policies, leader behaviors also have an outsized effect on climate. Leadership style, for example, has been found to impact climate in ways that you might expect. A high-leader goal orientation helps promote a climate of goal setting. A servant-leadership orientation where managers put employees' needs first and share power will be more likely to create a climate focused on fairness and justice.[49] Generally speaking, leaders who want to create a certain climate need to do two things: communicate those expectations and model the kind of behavior desired.

Riot did this as well, though perhaps to ill effect in some cases. One manager reportedly told a story about how deeply he was affected by a certain *World of Warcraft* raid, then instructed employees to illustrate their own passion by creating such a gaming experience for themselves if they didn't already have one on tap. In response to the Kotaku article detailing the company's organizational climate, one former employee wrote an alleged account of an offsite meeting where 160 hiring managers heard one of Riot's cofounders joke that "no doesn't necessarily mean no." Some of the assembled managers grimaced in response, but many in the audience found the double entendre hilarious.[50] *A strong climate isn't always a good climate.*

 ## Climate Change

To its credit, Riot seems to have recognized the problems with its climate and has begun efforts to change it for the better. In the months following the revelations, Riot set to work publicly apologizing, changing its hiring practices, refreshing its credos to emphasize diversity and inclusion, and even hiring its first chief diversity officer, Angela Roseboro, to oversee diversity and inclusion programs and ensure that these

values were included in broader corporate strategies. According to a public-facing statement about company values, Riot leadership set out to disassemble the idea that there is only one kind of "gamer" worth considering, and noted that if words like that "are misused or don't help us describe our vision for the future, we won't use them."[51] The company promised that it was launching investigations into the misconduct of its managers and that punishment would be meted out. There would be more training, especially for managers and those in charge of hiring and promotion. The company brought on new leadership to help them focus on their desired values of diversity and inclusion and created a larger team dedicated to that effort. The company's two cofounders even vowed to step down if they couldn't change things for the better over time.

Indeed, roughly one year after the initial story broke, Roseboro reported that the company had added two more women to its leadership team, implemented twelve thousand hours of diversity training, and formed partnerships with organizations like Girls Who Code and the Reboot Representation Coalition to increase its pipeline of diverse talent.[52] Riot took even more steps, Roseboro reported in a post to the company's webpage, adding more executives and consultants to help evaluate and improve its corporate culture and to hold its leadership team accountable for delivering on diversity and inclusion efforts. Roseboro also noted that she and her colleagues did a comprehensive review and overhaul of Riot's recruiting and hiring process to ensure that they "have the opportunity to attract talent from different backgrounds and perspectives."[53] Much effort has been applied to elevating Riot's culture, and based on follow-up reporting from Kotaku, many employees seem to be happy with the results.

If you want to take some lessons from this wild ride, here are some things that you might do to help shape whatever organizational climate you want, be it for diversity, service, safety, or anything else:

▶ Communicate often and clearly about what kinds of behaviors are expected, rewarded, or unacceptable.

▶ Model these behaviors yourself.

▶ Ensure that personnel policies and systems are in line with the climate you want, that they reward the behaviors you want to see, and that they don't also reward behaviors you don't want to see.

▶ Learn how to engage in what's called *transformational leadership* where you work with employees to sell them on your vision, inspire them to change, and support them along the way.

▶ Create greater group cohesion, social interaction, and greater team interdependencies when appropriate (recall the chapter on teams!).

▶ Don't pass gas directly on your employees. Just…don't. I can't believe I have to say this.

Conclusion

So there you have it. I hope by this point that you realize the many lessons about how to be an effective leader that you learned from video games—even if you didn't realize it at the time. And if you have gamers who work with you (and let's face it, who doesn't these days), I expect that you now have some better insight into how they think and what they respond to.

Human motivation is human motivation regardless of context, and examples of what gets people to work hard, get passionate, develop skills, get along, and share an understanding of how things should be done can be found in a variety of places. Since it's the same human psychology, it's not as much a leap to take what you find works in games and apply it to other endeavors. The designers of these games did it, and the same psychological and management principles are available for your use. It's just a matter of recognizing when those opportunities are present in a situation and then seizing them as I've described throughout this book.

I hope you're now open to thinking like a game designer and a game player in this way. I hope you never stopped, in fact. To paraphrase the wise old man from 1986's *The Legend of Zelda*, "It's dangerous to go alone." Take these neatly packaged descriptions of human psychology as applied to a relatable and memorable context, because being an effective leader and manager is hard work and can be overwhelming whether you're a veteran or a first-timer. It helps to have models of human behavior and thought to draw from, and putting them in a relatable context like video games will help you both remember how they work and make them understood to others.

To help you stay in the spirit and continue this line of thinking, I have created a website that acts as a companion for this book. You can find it at **psychology ofgames.com**. There, you can peruse hundreds of articles and other resources that I've written on this topic over the years. It's also a great place to get in touch with me. I look forward to seeing you there and hearing about how you've made your workplace more like a video game.

Acknowledgments

Thanks to everyone who helped me research this book and encouraged me to pursue this idea. Thanks to Matt Barney at LeaderAmp for tolerating all this psychology of games stuff and even finding value in it for our work together. Thanks to everyone who has ever visited psychologyofgames.com or downloaded one of my podcasts. And thanks specifically to my Patreon supporters:

Arty Abe

Ferenc Acs

Jonathan Adams

James Alexander

Brian Anderson

Jose Arechavala

Clinton Balmain

Jen Barrick

Stephen Blessing

Paul Borawski

Brad Brook

Dorian Broski

Mark Buchholz

Alexandre da Silva
  Cavalcante

Yen Chang

Jakub Cikala

Jesse Clark

Michael Cole

Nick Creevey

Raphael D'Amico

Mark Dion

CB Droege

Evan Engle

Ekaterina Ermolenko

Conor Farrell

Matthew Frederick

Eric Frey

Caitlin Geier

Randy Greenback

Eva Grillova

Cameron H.

Darius Hansley

Sarah Hays

Pete Howell

Kaiyu Hsu

Alarion Irisar

Sebastian Rask Jepsen

Amanda Jørgensen

Tapani Joelsson

Gina Johnson

Zack Johnson

Jean-Stephane Jokeit

David Joyner

Nick Kartsanis

Kirill Krayushkin

Corey L

Raphaël Leroy

JM

Piotr Maciejewski

Rasul Majid	Vimal Tiwari
Jeff Matick	Shane Tilton
Artur Mittelbach	Michael Vieths
David C Morris	Arina Wagner
Pete Muller	Chi Wang
Gabrielle Ostrognay	Ed White
Jason Pace	Nathan Atlas Williams
Coral Page	Sarah Wilson
Gerry Paquette	William Winters
Todd Parsons	Bruce Woodward
Pira Pewnim	Chihiro Yamada
Cédric Plessis	Juha Ylimäki
Scott Reynolds	Dioneira
Mike Roberts	Caleb
Zack Roman	Matthew
Eric Rose	Gracek
Matthew Seaward	Paul
Peter Sienkowski	Arcturus
Jørund Skaug	Gordon
Sarah Tilley	Harry

Notes

1   Charlie Hall, "One Player Spent 10 Years Exploring Every Corner of Eve Online," Polygon, April 2, 2019, https://www.polygon .com/2019/4/2/18286977/eve-online-explorer-10-year-journey -katia-sae.

2   W. H. Macey and B. Schneider, "The Meaning of Employee Engagement," *Industrial and Organizational Psychology* 1, no. 1 (2008): 3–30, https://doi.org/10.1111/j.1754-9434.2007.0002.x.

3   W. H. Macey, B. Schneider, K. Barbera, and S. Young, *Employee Engagement: Tools for Analysis, Practice, and Competitive Advantage* (Malden, MA: Wiley-Blackwell, 2009).

4   A. K. Przybylski, S. C. Rigby, and R. M. Ryan, "A Motivational Model of Video Game Engagement," *Review of General Psychology* 14, no. 2 (2010): 154–166, https://doi.org/10.1037 /a0019440.

5   K. Beck, "'God of War' Breaks Sales Records for the PlayStation 4," Mashable, May 3, 2018, https://mashable.com/2018/05/03/god-of-war-sales/#bkCWQNtkXPqX.

6   E. A. Locke and G. P. Latham, *A Theory of Goal Setting & Task Performance* (Englewood Cliffs, NJ: Prentice-Hall, Inc., 1990).

7   E. A. Locke and G. P. Latham, *New Developments in Goal Setting and Task Performance* (New York: Routledge, 2012).

8   G. H. Seijts and G. P. Latham, "The Effect of Distal Learning, Outcome, and Proximal Goals on a Moderately Complex Task," *Journal of Organizational Behavior* 22 (2001): 291–307.

9   M. S. Taylor, C. D. Fisher, and D. R. Ilgen, "Individuals' Reactions to Performance Feedback in Organizations: A Control Theory Perspective," in *Research in Personnel and Human Resources Management*, ed. K. M. Rowland and G. R. Ferris (Greenwich, CT: JAI Press, 1984), 2: 81–124.

10   V. J. Shute, "Focus on Formative Feedback," *Review of Educational Research* 78, no. 1 (2008): 153–189, https://doi.org/10.3102/0034654307313795.

11   A. N. Kluger and A. DeNisi, "The Effects of Feedback Interventions on Performance: A Historical Review, a Meta-Analysis, and a Preliminary Feedback Intervention Theory," *Psychological Bulletin* 119, no. 2 (1996): 254–284, https://doi.org/10.1037/0033-2909.119.2.254.

12   Max Nisen, "Why GE Had to Kill Its Annual Performance Reviews after More Than Three Decades," *Quartz,* August 13, 2015, https://qz.com/428813/ge-performance-review-strategy-shift/.

13   T. Amabile and S. Kramer, *The Progress Principle: Using Small Wins to Ignite Joy, Engagement, and Creativity at Work* (Boston: Harvard Business School Publishing, 2011).

14   M. Sterry, "The Totalitarian Buddhist Who Beat Sim City," Vice, May 10, 2010, https://www.vice.com/en_us/article/4w4kg3/the -totalitarian-buddhist-who-beat-sim-city.

15   tasrhgs02, "SIMCITY 3000—MAGNASANTI—6 MILLION— ABSOLUTE MAXIMUM," YouTube Video, 6:59, July 25, 2010, https://www.youtube.com/watch?v=NTJQTc-TqpU.

16   Carol S. Dweck, *Mindset: The New Psychology of Success* (New York: Ballantine Books, 2006).

17   Carol S. Dweck, "How Companies Can Profit from a Growth Mindset," *Harvard Business Review* (2014): 28–29.

18   M. M. Lombardo and R. W. Eichinger, "High Potentials as High Learners," *Human Resource Management* 39 (2000): 321–329.

19   "Potential: Who's Doing What to Identify Their Best?" New Talent Management Network, 2015, https://www.talentstrategygroup .com/application/third_party/ckfinder/userfiles/files/NTMN%20 Potential%20Study%202015.pdf.

20 K. P. De Meuse, "Learning Agility: Its Evolution as a Psychological Construct and Its Empirical Relationship to Leader Success," *Consulting Psychology Journal* 69, no. 4 (2017): 267–295, https://doi.org/10.1037/cpb0000100.

21 D. Hoff and W. Burke, *Learning Agility: The Key to Leader Potential* (Tulsa, OK: Hogan Press, 2017).

22 V. H. Medvec, S. F. Madey, and T. Gilovich, "When Less Is More: Counterfactual Thinking and Satisfaction among Olympic Medalists," *Journal of Personality and Social Psychology* 69, no. 4 (1995): 603–610, https://doi.org/10.1037/0022-3514.69.4.603.

23 R. N. Landers, K. N. Bauer, and R. C. Callan, "Gamification of Task Performance with Leaderboards: A Goal Setting Experiment," *Computers in Human Behavior* 71 (2017): 508–515. https://doi.org/10.1016/j.chb.2015.08.008.

24 Landers, Bauer, and Callan, "Gamification of Task Performance," 513.

25 G. Goethals and J. Darley, "Social Comparison Theory: An Attributional Approach," in *Social Comparison Processes: Theoretical and Empirical Perspectives*, ed. J. Suls and R. Miller (Washington, DC: Hemisphere, 1977): 259–278.

26 M. D. Alicke, E. Zell, and D. L. Bloom, "Mere Categorization and the Frog-pond Effect," *Psychological Science : A Journal of the American Psychological Society/APS* 21, no. 2 (2010): 174–177.

27 B. D. G. Pope and M. E. Schweitzer, "Is Tiger Woods Loss Averse? Persistent Bias in the Face of Experience, Competition, and High Stakes," *American Economic Review* 101 (2011): 129–157.

28 S. M. Garcia, A. Tor, and R. Gonzalez, "Ranks and Rivals: A Theory of Competition," *Personality & Social Psychology Bulletin* 32, no. 7 (2006): 970–982, https://doi.org/10.1177/0146167206287640.

29 R. A. Guzzo and M. W. Dickson, "Teams in Organizations: Recent Research on Performance and Effectiveness," *Annual Review of Psychology* 47, no. 1 (2002): 307–338, https://doi.org/10.1146/annurev.psych.47.1.307.

30 A. V. Carron and L. R. Brawley, "Cohesion: Conceptual and Measurement Issues," *Small Group Research* 43, no. 6 (2012): 726–743, https://doi.org/10.1177/1046496412468072.

31 D. J. Beal, R. R. Cohen, M. J. Burke, and C. L. McLendon, "Cohesion and Performance in Groups: A Meta-Analytic Clarification of Construct Relations," *Journal of Applied Psychology* 88, no. 6 (2003): 989–1004, https://doi.org/10.1037/0021-9010.88.6.989.

32 B. Mullen and C. Copper, "The Relation between Group Cohesiveness and Performance: An Integration," *Psychological Bulletin* 115, no. 2 (2005): 210–227, https://doi.org/10.1037/0033-2909.115.2.210.

33 J. E. Mathieu, P. T. Gallagher, M. A. Domingo, and E. A. Klock, "Embracing Complexity: Reviewing the Past Decade of Team Effectiveness Research," *Annual Review of Organizational Psychology and Organizational Behavior* 6, no. 1 (2018): 17–46, https://doi.org/10.1146/annurev-orgpsych-012218-015106.

34 Mullen and Copper, "Relation."

35 M. A. Hogg, "Group Cohesiveness: A Critical Review and Some New Directions," *European Review of Social Psychology* 4, no. 1 (1993): 85–111, https://doi.org/10.1080/14792779343000031.

36 B. P. Indik, "Operational Size and Member Participation: Some Empirical Tests of Alternative Explanations," *Human Relation* 18 (1965): 339–350.

37 Beal et al., "Cohesion and Performance."

38 L. A. DeChurch and J. R. Mesmer-Magnus, "The Cognitive Underpinnings of Effective Teamwork: A Meta-Analysis," *Journal of Applied Psychology* 95, no. 1 (2010): 32–53, https://doi.org/10.1037/a0017328.

39 J. E. Mathieu, T. S. Heffner, G. F. Goodwin, K. Hobson, K. Ivory, M. Trip, and N. Windefelder, "The Influence of Shared Mental Models on Team Process and Performance," *Journal of Applied Psychology* 85, no. 2 (2000): 273–283, https://doi.org/10.l037t/0021-9010.85.2.273.

40 C. N. Lacerenza, S. L. Marlow, S. I. Tannenbaum, and E. Salas, "Team Development Interventions: Evidence-based Approaches for Improving Teamwork," *American Psychologist* 73, no. 4 (2018): 517–531, https://doi.org/10.1037/amp0000295.

41 J. Sue, "Culture Clash: Why Arena of Valor is Struggling in America," Games Industry, August 10, 2018, https://www.gamesindustry.biz/articles/2018-08-10-culture-clash-why-arena-of-valor-is-struggling-in-america.

42 J. Madigan, *Getting Gamers: The Psychology of Video Games and Their Impact on the People Who Play Them* (New York: Rowman & Littlefield, 2015).

43 C. D'Anastasio, "Inside the Culture of Sexism at Riot Games," Kotaku, August 7, 2018, https://kotaku.com/inside-the-culture-of-sexism-at-riot-games-1828165483.

44 C. D'Anastasio, "The State of California Is Investigating Riot Games for Gender Discrimination," Kotaku, June 12, 2019, https://kotaku.com/the-state-of-california-is-investigating-riot-games-for-1835463823.

45 B. Schneider, M. G. Ehrhart, and W. Macey, "Organizational Climate and Culture," *Annual Review of Psychology* 64 (2013): 361–388, https://doi.org/10.1146/annurev-psych-1130 11-143809.

46 M. G. Ehrhart, B. Schneider, and W. H. Macey, *Organizational Climate and Culture: An Introduction to Theory, Research, and Practice* (New York: Routledge, 2014).

47 B. Crecente, "'League of Legends' Developer Gears Up for Next Big Game," *Variety*, August 2, 2018, https://variety .com/2018/gaming/features/riot-games-next-game-league-of -legends-1202892072/.

48 M. S. Christian, J. C. Bradley, J. C. Wallace, and M. J. Burke, "Workplace Safety: A Meta-Analysis of the Roles of Person and Situation Factors," *Journal of Applied Psychology* 94, no. 5 (2009): 1103–1127, https://doi.org/10.1037/a0016172.

49 M. G. Ehrhart, "Leadership and Procedural Justice Climate as Antecedents of Unit-Level Organizational Citizenship Behavior," *Personnel Psychology* 57, no. 1 (2004): 61–94.

50 B. Hawkins, "The Story of Why I Left Riot Games," August 27, 2018, http://barryhawkins.com/blog/posts/the-story-of-why-i-left -riot-games/.

51 "Our First Steps Forward," Riot Games, August 29, 2018, https:// www.riotgames.com/en/who-we-are/our-first-steps-forward.

52 C. D'Anastasio, "Riot Employees Say Company Has Made Real Progress Fixing Its Sexism Issues," Kotaku, August 7, 2019, https://kotaku.com/riot-games-and-sexism-one-year-later -1837041215.

53 A. Roseboro, "Riot Games One Year Later: My Reflections," Riot Games, August 6, 2019, https://www.riotgames.com/en/news /riot-one-year-later-my-reflections.

About the Author

JAMIE MADIGAN, PhD, has become an expert on the psychology of video games and seeks to popularize understanding of how psychology can be used to understand why games are made how they are and why their players behave as they do. Dr. Madigan also writes, podcasts, and lectures on the subject for various magazines, websites, and his own site at psychologyofgames.com. He has consulted with game development companies and talked at conferences about how game developers can incorporate psychology principles into game design and how players can understand how it affects their play. He is the Head of Product at LeaderAmp.com, which offers science and technology to scale leadership coaching.

NEW! Only from Simple Truths®

IGNITE READS
spark impact in just one hour

IGNITE READS IS A NEW SERIES OF 1-HOUR READS WRITTEN BY WORLD-RENOWNED EXPERTS!

These captivating books will help you become the best version of yourself, allowing for new opportunities in your personal and professional life. Accelerate your career and expand your knowledge with these powerful books written on today's hottest ideas.

TRENDING BUSINESS AND PERSONAL GROWTH TOPICS

 Read in an hour or less

 Leading experts and authors

 Bold design and captivating content

EXCLUSIVELY AVAILABLE ON SIMPLETRUTHS.COM

Need a training framework?
Engage your team with discussion guides and PowerPoints for training events or meetings.

Want your own branded editions?
Express gratitude, appreciation, and instill positive perceptions to staff or clients by adding your organization's logo to your edition of the book.

Add a supplemental visual experience
to any meeting, training, or event.

Contact us for special corporate discounts!
(800) 900-3427 x247 or
simpletruths@sourcebooks.com

LOVED WHAT YOU READ AND WANT MORE?

Sign up today and be the FIRST to receive advance copies of Simple Truths® NEW releases written and signed by expert authors. Enjoy a complete package of supplemental materials that can help you host or lead a successful event. This high-value program will uplift you to be the best version of yourself!

— SIMPLE TRUTHS —
ELITE CLUB
ONE MONTH. ONE BOOK. ONE HOUR.

Your monthly dose of motivation, inspiration, and personal growth.